IF FO

👤 _____

✉ _____

📱 _____

# Greater Than a Tourist Book Series Reviews from Readers

I think the series is wonderful and beneficial for tourists to get information before visiting the city.

-Seckin Zumbul, Izmir Turkey

I am a world traveler who has read many trip guides but this one really made a difference for me. I would call it a heartfelt creation of a local guide expert instead of just a guide.

-Susy, Isla Holbox, Mexico

New to the area like me, this is a must have!

 -Joe, Bloomington, USA

This is a good series that gets down to it when looking for things to do at your destination without having to read a novel for just a few ideas.

-Rachel, Monterey, USA

Good information to have to plan my trip to this destination.

-Pennie Farrell, Mexico


Great ideas for a port day.

-Mary Martin USA


Aptly titled, you won't just be a tourist after reading this book. You'll be greater than a tourist!

-Alan Warner, Grand Rapids, USA


Even though I only have three days to spend in San Miguel in an upcoming visit, I will use the author's suggestions to guide some of my time there. An easy read - with chapters named to guide me in directions I want to go.

 -Robert Catapano, USA


Great insights from a local perspective! Useful information and a very good value!

 -Sarah, USA


This series provides an in-depth experience through the eyes of a local. Reading these series will help you to travel the city in with confidence and it'll make your journey a unique one.

-Andrew Teoh, Ipoh, Malaysia

>TOURIST

# GREATER THAN A TOURIST- CHAUTAUQUA LAKE REGION NEW YORK USA

*50 Travel Tips from a Local*

R Peterson

Greater Than a Tourist- Chautauqua Lake Region New York USA Copyright © 2019 by CZYK Publishing LLC. All Rights Reserved.

All rights reserved. No part of this book may be reproduced in any form or by any electronic or mechanical means including information storage and retrieval systems, without permission in writing from the author. The only exception is by a reviewer, who may quote short excerpts in a review.

The statements in this book are of the authors and may not be the views of CZYK Publishing or Greater Than a Tourist.

Cover designed by: Ivana Stamenkovic
Cover Image: https://pixabay.com/en/lake-chautauqua-fluffy-clouds-2697146/

CZYK Publishing Since 2011.

Greater Than a Tourist
Visit our website at www.GreaterThanaTourist.com

Lock Haven, PA
All rights reserved.
**ISBN:** 9781793851161

# >TOURIST

## 50 TRAVEL TIPS FROM A LOCAL

>TOURIST

# BOOK DESCRIPTION

Are you excited about planning your next trip?

Do you want to try something new?

Would you like some guidance from a local?

If you answered yes to any of these questions, then this Greater Than a Tourist book is for you.

Greater Than a Tourist- Chautauqua Lake Region, New York State, United States by R Peterson offers the inside scoop on The Chautauqua Lake Region. Most travel books tell you how to travel like a tourist. Although there is nothing wrong with that, as part of the Greater Than a Tourist series, this book will give you travel tips from someone who has lived at your next travel destination.

In these pages, you will discover advice that will help you throughout your stay. This book will not tell you exact addresses or store hours but instead will give you excitement and knowledge from a local that you may not find in other smaller print travel books.

Travel like a local. Slow down, stay in one place, and get to know the people and the culture. By the time you finish this book, you will be eager and prepared to travel to your next destination.

>TOURIST

# TABLE OF CONTENTS

BOOK DESCRIPTION
TABLE OF CONTENTS
DEDICATION
ABOUT THE AUTHOR
HOW TO USE THIS BOOK
FROM THE PUBLISHER
OUR STORY
WELCOME TO
> TOURIST
INTRODUCTION
1. Pronunciation Basics
2. Spelling Chautauqua
3. The Top 4 Tips
4. Tip #1
5. Tips #2
6. Tip #3
7. Tip #4
8. Major Attractions
9. Major Attraction #1: The National Comedy Center
10. Major Attraction #2: Lucille Ball
11. Major Attraction #3: Lucy' Gravesite
12. Major Attraction #4: Lucille Ball Comedy Festival

13. Attraction #5: The Lucy-Desi Museum
14. Attraction #6: Chautauqua Institution
15. More Chautauqua Tips
16. Chautauqua Snobbery
17. One more note on Chautauqua and Titles
18. Attraction # 7: Robert H. Jackson Center
19. Attraction #8: Natalie Merchant's Hometown
20. Attraction #9: The Roger Tory Peterson Institute
21. The Biggest and Best Attraction: The Lake Itself
22. The Lake: A Little History
23. The Lake: What's Along Its Shores?
24. The Lake: The Best Vista
25. The Lake: A Closer Look
26. The Lake: Getting Up Close and Personal
27. The Lake: Boating and Fishing
28. Back to the Woods: The Chautauqua Gorge
29. The Woods: Panama Rocks
30. Trails: Fred J. Cusimano Westside Overland Trail
31. Trails: Chautauqua Rails to Trails
32. Directions and Transportation
33. Transportation: You Must Drive Everywhere to Get Anywhere
34. Directions: The Futility of the Grid
35. Directions: Looking Before You Leap (and Travel)
36. Communities Around the Lake: Jamestown

>TOURIST

37. Communities: Lakewood
38. Communities: Mayville
39. Communities: Bemus Point
40. Continuing the Lecture
41. Tip #5
42. Tip #6
43. Tip #7
44. Tip #8
45. Niche Attractions: Local History
46. Niche Attractions: Motorcycle Heaven
47. Niche Attractions: Music
48. Niche Attractions: Ice Cream!
49. Niche Attractions: Not Buffalo Wings—Just call them Chicken Wings
50. When (Not) To Come

TOP REASONS TO BOOK THIS TRIP

50 THINGS TO KNOW ABOUT PACKING LIGHT FOR TRAVEL

Packing and Planning Tips

Travel Questions

Travel Bucket List

NOTES

>TOURIST

## DEDICATION

This book is dedicated to every local who has ever moaned about slow drivers on Route 394, to every person who has driven slowly on Route 394, and to all those who will do so even after they read this guide. Ah well.

>TOURIST

## ABOUT THE AUTHOR

R Peterson grew up in the Chautauqua Lake Region. While doing so, she climbed a lot of trees, swam for countless hours in the lake, and ran through a lot of knee-high snow to catch the bus a quarter mile up the road from her house (through the woods). She has since lived abroad and in a major metropolitan American city. These experiences expanded her horizons but also refined the lines of her love for Chautauqua.

\>TOURIST

# HOW TO USE THIS BOOK

The Greater Than a Tourist book series was written by someone who has lived in an area for over three months. The goal of this book is to help travelers either dream or experience different locations by providing opinions from a local. The author has made suggestions based on their own experiences. Please do your own research before traveling to the area in case the suggested places are unavailable.

**Travel Advisories**: As a first step in planning any trip abroad, check the Travel Advisories for your intended destination.
https://travel.state.gov/content/travel/en/traveladvisories/traveladvisories.html

## FROM THE PUBLISHER

Traveling can be one of the most important parts of a person's life. The anticipation and memories that you have are some of the best. As a publisher of the Greater Than a Tourist book series, as well as the popular 50 Things to Know book series, we strive to help you learn about new places, spark your imagination, and inspire you. Wherever you are and whatever you do I wish you safe, fun, and inspiring travel.

Lisa Rusczyk Ed. D.
CZYK Publishing

>TOURIST

## OUR STORY

Traveling is a passion of the "Greater than a Tourist" series creator. Lisa studied abroad in college, and for their honeymoon Lisa and her husband toured Europe. During her travels to Malta, an older man tried to give her some advice based on his own experience living on the island since he was a young boy. She was not sure if she should talk to the stranger but was interested in his advice. When traveling to some places she was wary to talk to locals because she was afraid that they weren't being genuine. Through her travels, Lisa learned how much locals had to share with tourists. Lisa created the "Greater Than a Tourist" book series to help connect people with locals. A topic that locals are very passionate about sharing.

>TOURIST

# WELCOME TO
# > TOURIST

>TOURIST

# INTRODUCTION

"To Travel is to Live" – Hans Christian Andersen

The following 50 tips are for the tourist who wants a restful, low-impact vacation in the Chautauqua Lake Region. That is, low-impact for you, but also low-impact on the beautiful county you're visiting. Chautauqua County depends significantly on tourism for its economic survival. While once agricultural...well, how much more do I need to say? Small farms are hardly a robust part of the American economy anymore. Locals tolerate tourists, but we also chafe at your presence. However, we mostly complain about tourists who are blatantly inconsiderate towards ourselves and our home. So in conclusion: come! Yes, please come! But remember, you're visiting our house. Take off your shoes before you come in the living room. Observe the rules laid out for guests. Clean up after yourself. We appreciate it.

>TOURIST

# 1. PRONUNCIATION BASICS

It's pronounced "Sh"autauqua. Not "Ch"autauqua. "Tourist" is written on your forehead the moment you make this worn out mistake. This not only sounds wrong to locals, it sounds pretentious. Don't give yourself away so soon!

# 2. SPELLING CHAUTAUQUA

And yes, Chautauqua has three a's and three u's in it. Incredible. Hopefully, however, you won't need to spell it very often. If you do, just remember 'a' comes before 'u' except after 'q'.

# 3. THE TOP 4 TIPS

The following four tips reflect THE major peeves by current residents. They are informed by my own experience as well as by data-driven scientific analysis (well, I cross-referenced with fellow residents). These issues affect our commutes, our jobs, and even our children, so please consider observing them.

## 4. TIP #1

First and foremost--Don't drive slower than the posted speed limit. This appears to be the result of the area's scenic beauty, which is undoubtedly one of the biggest factors that keeps residents here (since, for instance, job opportunity is not). However, the beauty of the trees, the hills, and most of all the lake is not sufficient reason to drive 10 to 20 miles under the speed limit. This occurs most frequently on roadways running parallel to the lake. For one, driving 10-20 miles under the speed limit is dangerous! Moreover, it's also absolutely infuriating to get stuck behind someone when trying to get to work. So watch your speedometer! Drive the speed limit, please!

## 5. TIPS #2

Ironically, this second big tip is to slow down. Growing up on a dead end road leading towards the lake, it was obvious even as a kid that visitors like to zoom down to see what's going on. In addition to not particularly liking strangers gawking at our houses like they're on shelves at Target, locals especially don't appreciate speedy cars. These mini side trips for visitors are usually to residential side streets with, you

>TOURIST

know, things like kids on bikes, kids running around, pets, etc. As such, cars should be crawling: we're talking 5-10 mph. 15 max. It doesn't matter if there's no speed limit. Especially if there's no speed limit, please drive at snail pace. For the kids, the pets, and for your viewing pleasure.

# 6. TIP #3

Did I mention this county is historically agricultural? Lest I mislead you to believe that history's obsolete, turn down a road running perpendicular to the lake and you will comprehend how agricultural the county still is. Although there are swaths of suburban areas around the lake and the city of Jamestown perches at its southern tip, these suburban and urban residents have the same experience you do when you drive away from the lake--country, country, country. As a result, we're kinda earthy, crunchy people. All that to say, it's NOT a metropolitan area and locals are NOT cosmopolitan people. Do not expect fine French dining as a general rule. Exceptions exist, including fancy French cuisine you can pay a lot more for, but in general don't expect to receive high quality food from diners and chain restaurants. Expect diner food. Expect Applebees. Please stop critiquing apples by the standards of passionfruit.

## 7. TIP #4

Fourthly, and also about dining--Be patient with your servers. Especially teenagers. Regarding the latter, they wish you weren't there but know if you weren't they wouldn't have jobs. They're just going through the motions. Show them what graciousness and patience looks like. Most of the time they're working hard, doing their best. Remember what it was like to be 16 and work 40 hours a week during the summer? On your feet? Saving up for some treasured possession? Or college, so you could leave and get a better job somewhere where better jobs exist? Yeah, that's your server. Mostly likely. Keep that in mind.

## 8. MAJOR ATTRACTIONS

Alright. Now you know how to mind your manners, it's time to get back to why you want to come in the first place. The region has an endless

>TOURIST

number of awesome reasons you should come visit, from the obvious and advertised to the more subtle. We'll start with what you might have heard of and tell you a little more.

# 9. MAJOR ATTRACTION #1: THE NATIONAL COMEDY CENTER

This museum opened summer 2018, so as I write this it is still brand-spanking new. That's exciting news for you! For one, it means all the technological components of the museum--the interactive exhibits, the big screens--all that stuff still works. (As a lifelong museum fan, I'm telling you that stuff does not work for long and museums often don't have the money to maintain them). Notwithstanding frail technology, the museum will exist for a long time and fills a niche heretofore unrepresented in American museums: a national comedy museum. So it's pretty cool. Being created in the 21st century, it really covers everybody. Its missions states that the museum "celebrates comedy's great minds and unique voices, from Charlie Chaplin to Dave Chappelle." Lily Tomlin, Dan Aykroyd, and Amy Schumer were all present at its opening. Just keep in mind its high-profile merits come with the steepest price tag in town, too.

## 10. MAJOR ATTRACTION #2: LUCILLE BALL

There's lots to laugh about in Jamestown, NY, the small city where the Comedy Center is located. That's because the Center is the culmination of several events and museums that have existed in the area for some time. You might say it all started August 6, 1911. when Lucille Desiree Ball was born here, and Lucy was a small town girl who never forgot her roots. She made trips back to the area after gaining superstardom in Hollywood from her "I Love Lucy" show.

## 11. MAJOR ATTRACTION #3: LUCY' GRAVESITE

There are many ways to pay Lucy homage in the region. To start, you can pay your respects by visiting her grave in the beautiful Lake View Cemetery. The tree-lined paths of this cemetery are peaceful and

> TOURIST

quiet. Many of the stones are ornate and worth a pausing glance. Lucy's own situation in the cemetery is not overdone but obvious enough because there are signs leading to it. While initially buried in Forest-Lawn Hollywood Hills Cemetery in Los Angeles, Lucy's children moved her here in 2002. She now lies in a plot with her parents and grandparents.

# 12. MAJOR ATTRACTION #4: LUCILLE BALL COMEDY FESTIVAL

Lucy's comedic legacy had been celebrated in two major ways in the years leading up to the creation of the Comedy Center. As a child, I recall my mother, a redhead, dressing up as Lucy, climbing into a grape-filled barrel, and bringing the famous "I Love Lucy" episode "Lucy's Italian Movie" to life. This was part of the Lucille Ball Comedy Festival, an event born out of Lucy's own desire to see her hometown as a destination for comedy performance (versus a stale enshrinement of her own substantial legacy). Growing up, I saw billboards for stars like Jay Leno and Seinfeld participating in that same festival, although it did not involve the comedic giants stomping grapes (so far as I know). More recently, the Festival has attracted such high profile names as Trevor Noah, who, as you may know, replaced Jon Stewart on the Daily Show. The four-day festival takes place once a year and will likely become an even more seminal event in the region's calendar as the Comedy Center's reputation grows.

## 13. ATTRACTION #5: THE LUCY-DESI MUSEUM

The second precursor to the center was and is the Lucy Desi Museum. A much more traditional museum than the Center, it nonetheless is a great one, especially for those more particularly interested in the careers of Lucy and her husband, Desi Arnaz. The museum is full of costumes, props, and recreated sets from the I Love Lucy show. It also has more personal items related to the one-time king and queen of comedy, including portraits, never-before-seen footage, and reminiscences from Lucy's childhood friends.

>TOURIST

# 14. ATTRACTION #6: CHAUTAUQUA INSTITUTION

Interested in a more diverse and, at times, contemplative engagement with society? The second major attraction to the Chautauqua Lake Region is Chautauqua Institution. Established in 1873 as an instructional summer camp for Methodist Sunday school teachers, the Institution has since become much, much more. I find it difficult to explain precisely what it is to people, but I'll give it my best shot here. In short, the Institution is a summertime destination for enjoying the arts, religion, and intellectual discussion. Yet let it be said that this pithy description leaves out critically limiting aspects of the Institution. For instance, it's basically a gated community--you can't enter it without paying a fee. As a result, this is one of the most controversial attractions in the minds of residents--the county's economy benefits from it enormously; however, residents often cannot afford to access it for our own enjoyment. Notwithstanding this reality, you should enjoy it.

## 15. MORE CHAUTAUQUA TIPS

A few short tips for enjoying Chautauqua Institution (while maintaining relations with the locals): First, have I mentioned driving the speed limit? It is on the main roads leading towards Chautauqua Institution that I find visitors most inclined to adopt this most frustrating of habits. As I asked before I also ask now, again: please drive the speed limit.

## 16. CHAUTAUQUA SNOBBERY

The Institution is a prestigious place. However, in addition to existing as a result of the altruistic aspirations of men like co-founder and Methodist minister John Heyl Vincent, it was undeniably founded on the Industrial-Age moneyed interests of men like co-found and industrialist Lewis Miller. This aura of prestige has never left and, as any local will tell you, has morphed for many "Chautauquans" into snobbery. I could go on about this for awhile; suffice it to say, please don't be a snob.

>TOURIST

# 17. ONE MORE NOTE ON CHAUTAUQUA AND TITLES

Generally people who refer to themselves as "Chautauquans" are patrons of Chautauqua Institution. As a local, I have never referred to myself as such. Nor do I think most residents.

# 18. ATTRACTION # 7: ROBERT H. JACKSON CENTER

Though Lucy was undeniably world famous in her own right, and the Institution supports the humanistic vision of a global perspective, my favorite attraction of international historical significance is the Robert H. Jackson Center. Located in Jamestown, NY, the Center highlights the life and work of Robert H. Jackson, known foremost as the Chief United States Prosecutor at the Nuremberg Trials of Nazi war criminals in 1945/46. Held up as something of a humanitarian figure today, I am especially proud to be from the same county as this historic figure. For instance, of lesser renown but of equal consequence, while on the Supreme Court during WWII, Jackson dissented from the majority opinion of his fellow justices on the Korematsu v. United States decision, a decision which ultimately uphold deportation of Japanese citizens and legal immigrants to internment camps around the US. Jackson, like Lucille Ball, also maintained connections with the area, a testament to the region's draw on its locals. When Chief Jackson died, his funeral was held in Jamestown and all eight living justices attended.

## 19. ATTRACTION #8: NATALIE MERCHANT'S HOMETOWN

Well, maybe not precisely an attraction, per se, except for sake of pilgrimage. Though not, to my knowledge, connected to the region like her comedic and historic predecessors by any memorial or festival, Natalie Merchant is still alive!--so there's still a chance that something could eventually be established! Merchant is best known as lead singer of 10,000 Maniacs as well as for her successful career as a solo artist, singing 90s classics like "Kind and Generous". Merchant joined the band that would become the Maniacs while attending local Jamestown Community College. My favorite thing we have in common is encapsulated in the following quote, which I very well could have said myself: "As a young girl...it was my favorite place...I spent countless hours between the shelves of [Prendergast] library. I remember being absolutely overwhelmed by what they contained." As such, this large city library is, perhaps, the most reasonable place of pilgrimage to sit and hum (very quietly) your favorite Natalie tune.

## 20. ATTRACTION #9: THE ROGER TORY PETERSON INSTITUTE

To round out our list of famous locals is Roger Tory Peterson. I can't speak for all residents of the region, but the natural beauty of the area does, I think, influence its residents to be nature lovers. This was certainly the case with Peterson. You may have heard of Audubon? Well, Peterson's right up there with him. Both were nature artists, Peterson for his field guides, which are reliable to this day, despite being painted (versus photographed) and first being published in 1934. For nature lovers, the Roger Tory Peterson Institute of Natural History is a great place to visit. The building is enormous--a testament to all

Peterson's multifaceted work. Many of the specimens he drew are stored in the institute as well as much of his artwork. Nestled in a wooded area with a few walking trails circling it, it's worth the modest price tag and donating a little extra as well.

## 21. THE BIGGEST AND BEST ATTRACTION: THE LAKE ITSELF

I'll get back to talking about the woods later--First, the lake itself should take its place as the heart of the Chautauqua Lake Region's natural world. This is undoubtedly the case for several reasons, foremost among them that the abundance of water it provides is the lifeblood of the region's ecosystems.

## 22. THE LAKE: A LITTLE HISTORY

The lake, which is NOT one of the Finger Lakes, was reputedly formed by a glacier retreating about 10,000 years ago (no eyewitnesses, you're just going to have to trust me). The glacier essentially formed two basins--the result is a long, thin lake that pinches in the middle. The upper half, near Jamestown, is quite shallow. The deepest point is in the middle, with the lower half, near Mayville, still deeper generally than the upper half. The first humans who utilized its bountiful resources were Native Americans, from whom we derive the name Chautauqua (though the particulars of the history of that name make for a whole lecture in and of itself, the likes of which I heard from a local at Chautauqua Institution).

## 23. THE LAKE: WHAT'S ALONG ITS SHORES?

The perimeter of the lake is mostly residential. As such, it's not really possible to just walk at the lake's edge to enjoy the view. In reality, you'd be trespassing through one private patch of property after another. I know this because I did it as a child; however, mostly when our neighbors--who were seasonal visitors--weren't there. As such, I don't encourage it for people who are, in fact, short-term visitors themselves.

# 24. THE LAKE: THE BEST VISTA

As it is not possible to simply walk at the lakeshore, it is helpful to know where the best public places are to take in the lake view. If you're looking for the grand vista, you're in luck. One appeared in the last 10 years; one that is, essentially, meant for you. A scenic overlook and rest stop off of Interstate-86 between exits 10 and 11, keep in mind it's only accessible on the east-bound route. It's a pretty good spot for sunsets. The location is perched atop one of the area's rolling hills.

# 25. THE LAKE: A CLOSER LOOK

One of the best places to take in the lake at close range (without paying for the pomp of Chautauqua Institution, which otherwise has a spectacular view along its lengthy shoreline) is Bemus Point. The village of Bemus Point. Yep, villages still exist and this one lives up to a lot of the quaintness we attribute to such a designation. Long a tourist destination, Bemus Point provides a beautiful, albeit rather short walk, along the lakeside. Start where Main Street meets the waterfront (that is, the restaurant adjacent to it). Turn left. Walk along the water. The sidewalk is wide, the docks are picturesque, and the whole thing is set off especially well by an ice cream cone in hand. But cross your fingers--the whole experience is much pleasanter if the smell of dead fish is not present. Unfortunately, there's not a lot anyone can do about that. In any case, continue walking toward the historic Casino Restaurant (which is not a casino). More ice cream is available there (stay tuned for more information about delicious local ice cream stands).

## 26. THE LAKE: GETTING UP CLOSE AND PERSONAL

Of course, you may not only want to look at the lake--you may want to be on it, or even in it. Here are some basics about your close encounters of the lake kind. First, it's a lake. It's not the ocean, it's not a chlorine pool, it's not...whatever else you might expect it to be. Your bathtub? Not only is it a lake, it is a eutrophying lake. What does that mean? Well, it means that it's not exactly a sparkly, clear lake either. Ever since I was a child, one of the biggest problems the lake has had is weeds. While weeds are relatively normal in large bodies of water, the amount and kind is actually very indicative of the health of the lake. Our lake, well…it's got lots of weeds of the wrong variety. First, the flow of organic matter into the lake, escalated by humans and including everything rainfall brings to the lake's shores, ramps up the speed at which stuff grows in it. Weeds, for example. Lots of them. Second, the transfer of boats from lake to lake has led to the an infestation of invasive species of weeds, which choke the good stuff and encourage the bad stuff and, well—you get the picture. The point is, it's still safe to swim. But remember! It is not the ocean. It is not a chlorine pool. It is not your bathtub. But it is water. And it feels great in the summer.

## 27. THE LAKE: BOATING AND FISHING

Boating and fishing are very popular and enjoyable activities many locals and visitors enjoy on the lake. BYOB? Sure, bring your own boat, from your row boat to your motor boat, even a houseboat. The lake is big, deep, and there are generally not as many restrictions on motor boats as there are on smaller lakes. There are boat launches located around the lake at various locations, including public ones.

>TOURIST

There are also places you can dock your boat (for a reasonable fee) such that it is possible to use your boat to travel around the lake to places like Bemus Point and Chautauqua Institution. Because the lake is large--17 miles long and as much as two miles wide--the lake never feels terribly congested. That is, you can zip along with skiers or tubers behind you to great effect without great concern, although being a smart, watchful captain remains as necessary as in any boating situation. Because the lake isn't too large, it's also a great spot for the more demure canoer or kayaker, especially in the morning when the lake is usually pretty placid. Morning, and evening too, are also great times for fishing. The lake is known for its walleye as well as perch, sunfish, and, most excitingly, muskellunge or muskie. I know--I've caught or seen someone else catch each of them.

## 28. BACK TO THE WOODS: THE CHAUTAUQUA GORGE

And now, back to the woods. Chautauqua County is a beautifully wooded area of gently rolls hills that dip, ultimately, towards our own lake as well as to the lowlands adjacent to Lake Erie and to the peaks of the

Alleghenies to the southeast. Because of the area's glacial inheritance, there are also some unique areas whose rock forms stand out from the usual pattern of the region. Chief among these are the Chautauqua Gorge and Panama Rocks. The Gorge is, well, a gorge--a rock formation of high walls bordering a creek. As a NYS park, it's free and only a 10 minute drive west from Mayville at the lower end of the lake. It's a great place to hike then have a picnic lunch, as is Panama Rocks. Overall the hiking's pretty mild, fun for families or just taking a woodland stroll. Hiking boots are a good idea, though. As is bug spray.

## 29. THE WOODS: PANAMA ROCKS

Panama Rocks is located further south but still only a 15 minute drive from the lake. According to its website, that park (which has a small fee) is "reputed to be the most extensive formations of glacier-cut, ocean-quartz conglomerate in the world, forming a ridge half a mile long." That should sound impressive. Although not as spectacular in scale or peculiarity as what you will find out West, it is

> TOURIST

nonetheless pretty cool. Plus it's green. So green! Dark, deep, emerald-satisfying green. Ahhhhhh.

## 30. TRAILS: FRED J. CUSIMANO WESTSIDE OVERLAND TRAIL

For the hardier hiker there are two options. First is the Fred J. Cusimano Westside Overland Trail. This trail is 23.6 miles long in total. It runs continuously west some miles west of Chautauqua Lake. Of what I have seen, it showcases quintessential hiking conditions of the area, which is to say nothing to crazy. To put it another way, you can make the trail as easy or as hard as you like. You can travel one leg of it and call it a day. You can do the whole thing to challenge yourself. You can dally along the way, or push yourself hard to work up a sweat. Either way you will soak up the beautiful northeastern forest ambiance so many enjoy about this region's natural offerings.

# 31. TRAILS: CHAUTAUQUA RAILS TO TRAILS

This collection of trails offers more built-in variety on the basis of a simple premise: former railroads turned into trails for recreational use. Unlike the Cusimano Trail, the R-T experience is best understood as several trails umbrellaed by the concept of rails to trails. As such, it's a good idea to study the maps before you go (I know I did). Unlike the Cusimano Trail, which is primarily wooded, the R-T trails vary from woodland to wetland to meadow. Their greatest benefit is their wide, flat paths, which are more conducive to running and bicycling than the narrower, sometimes rooted and rocky paths of the Cusimano Trail. Individual legs of the R-T trails range from a 0.5 miles to 5 miles.

# 32. DIRECTIONS AND TRANSPORTATION

Talking about trails makes me think of directions and transportation, an important consideration when visiting anyplace new. As in most places in the US, the paths by which people travel the contours of the Chautauqua Lake Region has changed a great deal in the last 100 years. For instance, I am astounded by how much the lake itself was used as a critical form of transportation before the advent of the car. Alas for the paddlewheel boat and the ferry (although one of each still exists on the lake)! The most recent major change to the lake's circuits was the addition of the Chautauqua County Veterans Memorial Bridge in 1982. Driving over this bridge also provides one of the most beautiful views of the lake; however, as I mentioned before (perhaps several times at this point), driving more slowly in order to take in the view is prohibitive to all driver's safety, especially on the bridge where the speed limit is 65 mph.

## 33. TRANSPORTATION: YOU MUST DRIVE EVERYWHERE TO GET ANYWHERE

The most fundamental fact of transportation in the area is that you must drive everywhere. Public transit does not exist. Bicycles are fun but only useful as transit for cycling enthusiasts in spandex. Walking won't get you anywhere in terms of getting from Point A to Point B. However, because the region is a small, lightly populated area, you will likely never be at a loss for parking and most of the time it will be free.

## 34. DIRECTIONS: THE FUTILITY OF THE GRID

As for directions, North, East, South, and West are not going to get you very far. The truth is that the lake is the major geographic marker and it does not run in a way that promotes using cardinal directions. Frankly, lake-oriented directional tips derive from this single question: can you point in the direction you think the lake is? Some people can figure this out, some can't. My sister, for instance, lived in the area her entire life. One day when we were driving on a road I thought was self-evidently parallel to the lake, I happened to ask her this critical question. To my surprise, she pointed off in a decidedly inaccurate direction. Don't worry. Google Maps is real. And it works in our region. We don't have that much nature.

>TOURIST

# 35. DIRECTIONS: LOOKING BEFORE YOU LEAP (AND TRAVEL)

Let me repeat, cardinal directions are not particularly useful in navigating the Chautauqua Lake Region. Landmarks are. The most useful ones besides the lake are the communities around the lake. Reviewing these on a map and getting an idea of what each offers will go a long way in helping you navigate quickly and successfully. Give them a look on a real map before coming. Seeing their relation to each other and the lake will streamline your on-location travel.

# 36. COMMUNITIES AROUND THE LAKE: JAMESTOWN

Start with the following four communities. First is Jamestown. Jamestown is as big as it gets in the region with a population of 30,000 and shrinking. Named for a different James than Virginia's famous first settlement (theirs after King James of England, ours after first settler James Prendergast), Jamestown is where you'll find a lot of the attractions listed at the beginning of this guide, including the Comedy Center, the Lucy-Desi Museum, the Robert H. Jackson Center, and the Roger Tory Peterson Institute. Jamestown is one of the few places where you can walk around and feel like you're getting somewhere, although the on-the-ground attractions are, at this time, still somewhat sparse. Nonetheless, it has a cool, small-city feel that may appeal to some visitors. Located at the upper end of the lake, water flows from the lake into the Chadakoin River, which still flows through Jamestown today.

## 37. COMMUNITIES: LAKEWOOD

Following Route 394 out of Jamestown, one segues into the Village of Lakewood. When I was a kid, Lakewood was the up and coming place--it's where the mall and strip plazas appeared, drawing business away from Jamestown. Alas, it's now receiving its own comeuppance as a result of online shopping. In any case, with the plazas and mall with enormous parking lot, you'll know where you are if you're cruising along that main strip. Don't be fooled by all the concrete though--take a detour one road closer to the lake or out into the country and you'll have a lovely drive through Lakewood.

## 38. COMMUNITIES: MAYVILLE

At the opposite end of the lake from Jamestown is the Village of Mayville, the county seat. Tiny in comparison even to Jamestown, Mayville might be described as a country hamlet. It has one intersection that warrants traffic signals. Bordering this intersection is the county's court building as well as jail (there's an underground passage connecting the two, the likes of which, my dad often told me, might have saved JFK's accused assassin, Lee Harvey Oswald, from a premature death, as well as the country from more than a half century of mystery surrounding a deeply tragic moment).

## 39. COMMUNITIES: BEMUS POINT

Your final major marker is Bemus Point. This village (you'll notice we're 3 for 4 on villages) is a favorite for a lot of people, not least of them being mine or, very likely, yours. As mentioned earlier,

Bemus Point has been a tourist destination for a long time. Like a century. This is one of the reasons Bemus--as locals call it for short--is home to one of only two Victorian Era hotels around the lake. In Bemus it's the Lenhart with its fun, multi-colored rocking chairs on its lake-facing front porch (at Chautauqua Institution it's the Athenaeum, minus the rockers...I think). The tourism blooming in Bemus is decidedly absent in Mayville. That is, in the summer months; Bemus' tourism season is pretty clearly delineated as a summer season: late June to early August. Or maybe that's just the way it seemed for a high school student working during the summer. Remember the teenagers (Major Tip #4).

## 40. CONTINUING THE LECTURE

And on that note, a few last finger-waggings; that is, in which I urge you to be a good visitor and mind your manners. Having grown up in a tourist town and gone on to primarily work jobs oriented towards the visiting public, I have intimately experienced the benefit of wages earned from visitor dollars and the frustrations endowed by those dollars. But my first experiences occurred in the Chautauqua Lake Region. The truth is, tourism is a growing industry that is expanding to every corner of the earth. It's a product of globalism and capitalism. Although a rebel at times, I'm no revolutionary. I'm not suggesting we topple the system. However, I strongly urge tourists to commit to a view of tourism as a chance to know our global neighbors better and build relationships. Tourism stripped of these elements is consumerism. Unlike grocery shopping, tourism is consumption not only of a product but of a place, and, in terms of labor, people. As such, the following are a few examples of what to do in order to not devour the locals of the Chautauqua County Region.

# 41. TIP #5

Don't just go to Wegmans to buy all your groceries. A habit typical of the "Chautauquans" of Chautauqua Institution, I urge all visitors to consider this tip. Wegmans is the Wholefoods or Trader Joe's of the area. Of course, I know locals who swear by it, too. But we're not talking about locals here, we're talking about you, the visitor. As someone bringing in substantial resources to the area, consider dispersing your grocery money elsewhere. Local is really better, and the options are many in the region. From spring to fall, farm stands, etc. offer fruits, vegetables, eggs, baked goods, and more. They're not hard to find-- homemade signs dot the roads, including many of the major ones around the lake. I promise, you'll see them even if you're going the speed limit.

## 42. TIP #6

And don't limit yourself to the stands. Buy basic groceries at small grocery stores. Like I said, spread out your where you spend. Not only will you feel "closer to the ground" but you will meet more people, have more fun, have more varied experiences, and support the local economy more meaningfully.

## 43. TIP #7

My second point is more essential and the most deeply personal: Don't buy property on the lake for seasonal use. That is to say, don't buy it to own. When you do this, you take the land away from full-time residents. It may also destroy the opportunity to preserve the land in its natural state. I grew up on a dead end road next to the lake and for the majority of my life, and even to this day, only two homes out of 15+ were and are now inhabited year-round. The others primarily see use for brief spates in the summer and around holidays like Christmas and New Years. I comprehend, though not fully, the benefits of having such property owners in the regions; however, I cannot believe that the breaks in community life absent houses produce is holistically beneficial to the larger residential community.

## 44. TIP #8

In lieu of property ownership, my suggestions are these: Rent. Stay at a bed and breakfast. Stay at one of two Victorian Era hotels. Camp. Yes, really. Okay, or maybe buy a small, pre-existing house. But let your footprint match the time you spend in the area and the level of interaction you intend to have with the local community.

# 45. NICHE ATTRACTIONS: LOCAL HISTORY

Okay, okay, that's the last of the finger shaking like my grandma used to do. We'll end here with some of the area's niche attractions, which happen to be some of my favorites. First, local history. The more I learn about Chautauqua, the more I appreciate it. I think it is truly an incredibly exemplary and very significant place in American history. Of course, the area was first home to several Native American groups. Being on the eastern seaboard, the county was a stage to early interactions between Natives and European explorers--stories yet unknown that movies could be made about, I'm sure. The area is also exemplary as an early American community--not colonial, but American as in post-1776. At that time the country was still young and the first settlers of European descent were pioneers--in western NY! The wild west was at our doorstep. By the second half of the 1800s, the region around the lake was an idyllic tourist area with steamers crisscrossing the lake's surface. At the same time as its wealthier inhabitants enjoyed the fun and luxury the lake could offer, immigrants came to the area to stake out a living. For example, men and women from Sweden settled in large numbers in Jamestown, bringing with them a skill for furniture-making that caused some to call the city "the Furniture Capital of the World." The county suffered with the rest of the country through WWII, but intriguingly--as I learned only this past summer--played host to prisoner of war camps, first for Italians and later for Germans. And yet unlike many a podunk place in America, in the 20th century the county produced not one but several internationally famous individuals, chief among them Lucille Ball, Robert H. Jackson, and Roger Tory Peterson. All these rabbit holes and more await your curiosity in the Chautauqua Lake Region.

## 46. NICHE ATTRACTIONS: MOTORCYCLE HEAVEN

One form of transportation I forgot to mention is the motorcycle. How could I forget? Western NY is a motorcyclist's dream! Did I mention the gently rolling hills? The attractive green trees, farms, fields, and meadows? And there's little to no traffic! Even in the busy areas! (Well, except that one thoroughfare in Lakewood). But those aren't the areas you want to be with your motorcycle anyway. As I've said, drive perpendicularly away from the lake and "Boom!" you're in motorcycle heaven. Two-lane, usually double-lined paved roads lead into that lovely agricultural or wooded oasis that is western NY. Drive and drive and drive and drive. It's absolutely beautiful. And you'll usually find an ice cream stand as an excuse for a tasty pit stop, even in the smallest villages. Especially there, actually.

## 47. NICHE ATTRACTIONS: MUSIC

As I look back on the benefits of growing up in Chautauqua, one of the things that jumps out at me is music. We had good music. Good music programs in the schools, good music opportunities for students, and access to pretty incredible levels of musicianship within the community. This was in no small part due to Chautauqua Institution, which during its 9-week summer program is host to its own symphony orchestra, opera and theatre companies, chamber music performances, and various programs for extremely talented young adult musicians. All that on top of popular music performances throughout the summer. And then there's the sacred music, perhaps even at the heart of the music program: the music of choirs, congregations, and the 1907 Massey Memorial Organ nestled within the 5,000 seat Amphitheatre. However, the high caliber of music cannot be wholly attributed to the Institution. And yet, I don't know exactly what lies underneath the rest of it, connecting the various strands to bring out the best. All I know is it was and is there. In the schools. In the churches. In the bars where small bands play. In our hearts. Maybe you'll hear it, too.

## 48. NICHE ATTRACTIONS: ICE CREAM!

And if you don't hear that music, well...there's ice cream! Have I mentioned ice cream yet? Ah! Quite possibly my favorite part of re-visiting home when I have lived elsewhere is coming back for ice cream. What is better than a cheap ice cream cone from the window of a tiny shack? Good ice cream! It may be cheap, but it's good! Of course, when I say cheap I mean in contrast to metropolitan areas. I once got a small cone from JP Licks, a chain established in Boston known for its unique and quality flavors, for $7.00. Yes, really!! I got the chocolate-dipped cone, but still! In Chautauqua, you can get a small cone for as little as $3.25 (2018 dollars) including tax. Now, that doesn't include chocolate dipped cones or anything, but here's the facts: you get a ton of ice cream and you get great ice cream. Creamy, hard ice cream. Well, there's soft serve, too. In fact, a couple places specialize in all kinds of soft serve. But the best are hard! 3D Chocolate; Chocolate Chip Cookie Dough; Eskimo Kisses; Tiramisu; Peanut Butter Pretzel; Salty Jack; Moose Tracks; Piece of Cake! These flavors primarily represent two brands, Hershey's and Perry's; however, there's more! Stands are located all around the lake and include favorites like the Bemus Market in Bemus Point, Boxcar Barney's in Mayville, and Big Tree Soft Serve in Lakewood (which serves all the fun soft serve flavors, but also does really excellent hard ice cream, too). Watch out for lines of baseball and soccer teams, but don't worry too much. Those teenage girls and guys scooping the ice cream are generally pros. I should know--it was my first job ever. Might have something to do with how much I still love ice cream.

>TOURIST

# 49. NICHE ATTRACTIONS: NOT BUFFALO WINGS—JUST CALL THEM CHICKEN WINGS

Lest you think ice cream is the only food item worth visiting the region for, let me tell you about my favorite food of all time: chicken wings. Not buffalo chicken wings. You see, if you're from western NY, you don't need that extra adjective. You just know. Glorious chicken wings. The sauce we're familiar with was developed in Buffalo by the Anchor Bar in 1964 (according to Wikipedia; as you can imagine, there are some discrepancies over the details). Traditionally, three flavors were offered: mild, medium, and hot. Mild is more buttery than hot and remains my favorite. Today, depending on the establishment you visit, many more flavors may be offered. But try the originals first! Dip them in some bleu cheese. Crunch a carrot stick or stalk of celery afterwards. Down it with some soda or beer. So good.

# 50. WHEN (NOT) TO COME

And for your final tip, I leave you with this critical piece of advice: Just don't visit between November and March. I'm serious. After trudging through the snow and cold to get to my bus stop for thirteen years, take my word for it. Visit us when the weather's nice. Better make it June through September. So please, come enjoy yourself. Just remember to take off your shoes before you come in the living room.

>TOURIST

# TOP REASONS TO BOOK THIS TRIP

Cool Stuff You Wouldn't Expect from Small town America: The

(First Ever) National Comedy Center (in the US); The Roger

Tory Peterson Nature Institute; Chautauqua Institution.

Nature: It is literally easy on the eyes. The green of the trees is
pleasant. The hills aren't too steep. The lake isn't too big. It's
just beautiful.

Ice Cream Cones: So delicious. Sigh. Have one every day.

>TOURIST

# BONUS BOOK

# 50 THINGS TO KNOW ABOUT PACKING LIGHT FOR TRAVEL

# PACK THE RIGHT WAY EVERY TIME

# AUTHOR: MANIDIPA BHATTACHARYYA

First Published in 2015 by Dr. Lisa Rusczyk. Copyright 2015. All Rights Reserved. No part of this publication may be reproduced, including scanning and photocopying, or distributed in any form or by any means, electronic or mechanical, or stored in a database or retrieval system without prior written permission from the publisher.

Disclaimer: The publisher has put forth an effort in preparing and arranging this book. The information provided herein by the author is provided "as is". Use this information at your own risk. The publisher is not a licensed doctor. Consult your doctor before engaging in any medical activities. The publisher and author disclaim any liabilities for any loss of profit or commercial or personal damages resulting from the information contained in this book.

Edited by Melanie Howthorne

## ABOUT THE AUTHOR

Manidipa Bhattacharyya is a creative writer and editor, with an education in English literature and Linguistics. After working in the IT industry for seven long years she decided to call it quits and follow her heart instead. Manidipa has been ghost writing, editing, proof reading and doing secondary research services for many story tellers and article writers for about three years. She stays in Kolkata, India with her husband and a busy two year old. In her own time Manidipa enjoys travelling, photography and writing flash fiction.

Manidipa believes in travelling light and never carries anything that she couldn't haul herself on a trip. However, travelling with her child changed the scenario. She seemed to carry the entire world with her for the baby on the first two trips. But good sense prevailed and she is again working her way to becoming a light traveler, this time with a kid.

>TOURIST

# INTRODUCTION

*He who would travel happily
must travel light.*

-Antoine de Saint-Exupéry

Travel takes you to different places from seas and mountains to deserts and much more. In your travels you get to interact with different people and their cultures. You will, however, enjoy the sights and interact positively with these new people even more, if you are travelling light.

When you travel light your mind can be free from worry about your belongings. You do not have to spend precious vacation time waiting for your luggage to arrive after a long flight. There is be no chance of your bags going missing and the best part is that you need not pay a fee for checked baggage.

People who have mastered this art of packing light will root for you to take only one carry-on, wherever you go. However, many people can find it really hard to pack light. More so if you are travelling with children. Differentiating between "must have" and "just in case" items is the starting point. There will be ample shopping avenues at your destination which are just waiting to be explored.

This book will show you 'packing' in a new 'light' – pun intended – and help you to embrace light packing practices for all of your future travels.

Off to packing!

# DEDICATION

I dedicate this book to all the travel buffs that I know, who have given me great insights into the contents of their backpacks.

# THE RIGHT TRAVEL GEAR

## 1. CHOOSE YOUR TRAVEL GEAR CAREFULLY

While selecting your travel gear, pick items that are light weight, durable and most importantly, easy to carry. There are cases with wheels so you can drag them along – these are usually on the heavy side because of the trolley. Alternatively a backpack that you can carry comfortably on your back, or even a duffel bag that you can carry easily by hand or sling across your body are also great options. Whatever you choose, one thing to keep in mind is that the luggage itself should not weigh a ton, this will give you the flexibility to bring along one extra pair of shoes if you so desire.

## 2. CARRY THE MINIMUM NUMBER OF BAGS

Selecting light weight luggage is not everything. You need to restrict the number of bags you carry as well. One carry-on size bag is ideal for light travel. Most carriers allow one cabin baggage plus one purse, handbag or camera bag as long as it slides under the seat in front. So technically, you can carry two items of luggage without checking them in.

## 3. PACK ONE EXTRA BAG

Always pack one extra empty bag along with your essential items. This could be a very light weight duffel bag or even a sturdy tote bag which takes up minimal space. In the event that you end up buying a lot of souvenirs, you already have a handy bag to stuff all that into and do not have to spend time hunting for an appropriate bag.

*I'm very strict with my packing and have everything in its right place. I never change a rule. I hardly use anything in the hotel room. I wheel my own wardrobe in and that's it.*

Charlie Watts

# CLOTHES & ACCESSORIES

## 4. PLAN AHEAD

Figure out in advance what you plan to do on your trip. That will help you to pick that one dress you need for the occasion. If you are going to attend a wedding then you have to carry formal wear. If not, you can ditch the gown for something lighter that will be comfortable during long walks or on the beach.

## 5. WEAR THAT JACKET

Remember that wearing items will not add extra luggage for your air travel. So wear that bulky jacket that you plan to carry for your trip. This saves space and can also help keep you warm during the chilly flight.

## 6. MIX AND MATCH

Carry clothes that can be interchangeably used to reinvent your look. Find one top that goes well with a couple of pairs of pants or skirts. Use tops, shirts and jackets wisely along with other accessories like a scarf or a stole to create a new look.

## 7. CHOOSE YOUR FABRIC WISELY

Stuffing clothes in cramped bags definitely takes its toll which results in wrinkles. It is best to carry wrinkle free, synthetic clothes or merino tops. This will eliminate the need for that small iron you usually bring along.

## 8. DITCH CLOTHES PACK UNDERWEAR

Pack more underwear and socks. These are the things that will give you a fresh feel even if you do not get a chance to wear fresh clothes. Moreover these are easy to wash and can be dried inside the hotel room itself.

## 9. CHOOSE DARK OVER LIGHT

While picking your clothes choose dark coloured ones. They are easy to colour coordinate and can last longer before needing a wash. Accidental food spills and dirt from the road are less visible on darker clothes.

## 10. WEAR YOUR JEANS

Take only one pair of Jeans with you, which you should wear on the flight. Remember to pick a pair that can be worn for sightseeing trips and is equally eloquent for dinner. You can add variety by adding light weight cargoes and chinos.

## 11. CARRY SMART ACCESSORIES

The right accessory can give you a fresh look even with the same old dress. An intelligent neck-piece, a couple of bright scarves, stoles or a sarong can be used in a number of ways to add variety to your clothing. These light weight beauties can double up as a nursing cover, a light blanket, beach wear, a modesty cover for visiting places of worship, and also makes for an enthralling game of peek-a-boo.

## 12. LEARN TO FOLD YOUR GARMENTS

Seasoned travellers all swear by rolling their clothes for compact and wrinkle free packing. Bundle packing, where you roll the clothes around a central object as if tying it up, is also a popular method of compact and wrinkle free packing. Stacking folded clothes one on top of another is a big no-no as it makes creases extreme and they are difficult to get rid of without ironing.

>TOURIST

## 13. WASH YOUR DIRTY LAUNDRY

One of the ways to avoid carrying loads of clothes is to wash the clothes you carry. At some places you might get to use the laundry services or a Laundromat but if you are in a pinch, best solution is to wash them yourself. If that is the plan then carrying quick drying clothes is highly recommended, which most often also happen to be the wrinkle free variety.

## 14. LEAVE THOSE TOWELS BEHIND

Regular towels take up a lot of space, are heavy and take ages to dry out. If you are staying at hotels they will provide you with towels anyway. If you are travelling to a remote place, where the availability of towels look doubtful, carry a light weight travel towel of viscose material to do the job.

## 15. USE A COMPRESSION BAG

Compression bags are getting lots of recommendation now days from regular travellers. These are useful for saving space in your luggage when you have to pack bulky dresses. While packing for the return trip, get help from the hotel staff to arrange a vacuum cleaner.

# FOOTWEAR

## 16. PUT ON YOUR HIKING BOOTS

If you have plans to go hiking or trekking during your trip, you will need those bulky hiking boots. The best way to carry them is to wear them on flight to save space and luggage weight. You can remove the boots once inside and be comfortable in your socks.

## 17. PICKING THE RIGHT SHOES

Shoes are often the bulkiest items, along with being the dainty if you are a female. They need care and take up a lot of space in your luggage. It is advisable therefore to pick shoes very carefully. If you plan to do a lot of walking and site seeing, then wearing a pair of comfortable walking shoes are a must. For more formal occasions you can carry durable, light weight flats which will not take up much space.

## 18. STUFF SHOES

If you happen to pack a pair of shoes, ensure you utilize their hollow insides. Tuck small items like rolled up socks or belts to save space. They will also be easy to find.

>TOURIST

# TOILETRIES

## 19. STASHING TOILETRIES

Carry only absolute necessities. Airline rules dictate that for one carry-on bag, liquids and gels must be in 3.4 ounce (100ml) bottles or less, and must be packed in a one quart zip-lock bag. If you are planning to stay in a hotel, the basic things will be provided for you. It's best is to buy the rest from the local market at your destination.

## 20. TAKE ALONG TAMPONS

Tampons are a hard to find item in a lot of countries. Figure out how many you need and pack accordingly. For longer stays you can buy them online and have them delivered to where you are staying.

## 21. GET PAMPERED BEFORE YOU TRAVEL

Some avid travellers suggest getting a pedicure and manicure just the day before travelling. This not only gives you a well kept look, you also save the trouble of packing nail polish. Remember, every little bit of weight reduced adds up.

# ELECTRONICS

## 22. LUGGING ALONG ELECTRONICS

Electronics have a large role to play in our lives today. Most of us cannot imagine our lives away from our phones, laptops or tablets. However while travelling, one must consider the amount of weight these electronics add to our luggage. Thankfully smart phones come along with all the essentials tools like a camera, email access, picture editing tools and more. They are smart to the point of eliminating the need to carry multiple gadgets. Choose a smart phone that suits all your requirements and travel with the world in your palms or pocket.

## 23. REDUCE THE NUMBER OF CHARGERS

If you do travel with multiple electronic devices, you will have to bear the additional burden of carrying all their chargers too. Check if a single charger can be used for multiple devices. You might also consider investing in a pocket charger. These small devices support multiple devices while keeping you charged on the go.

>TOURIST

## 24. TRAVEL FRIENDLY APPS

Along with smart phones come numerous apps, which are immensely helpful in our travels. You name it and you have an app for it at hand – take pictures, sharing with friends and family, torch to light dark roads, maps, checking flight/train times, find hotels and many other things. Use these smart alternatives to traditional items like books to eliminate weight and save space.

*I get ideas about what's essential
when packing my suitcase.*

-Diane von Furstenberg

## TRAVELLING WITH KIDS

## 25. BRING ALONG THE STROLLER

Kids might enjoy walking for a while but they soon tire out and a stroller is the just the right thing for them to rest in while you continue your tour. Strollers also double duty as a luggage carrier and shopping bag holder. Remember to pick a light weight, easy to handle brand of stroller. Better yet, find out in advance if you can rent a stroller at your destination.

## 26. BRING ONLY ENOUGH DIAPERS FOR YOUR TRIP

Diapers take up a lot of space and add to the weight of your luggage. Therefore it is advisable to carry just enough diapers to last through the trip and a few for afterwards, till you buy fresh stock at your destination. Unless of course you are travelling to a really remote area, in which case you have no choice but to carry the load. Otherwise diapers are something you will find pretty easily.

## 27. TAKE ONLY A COUPLE OF TOYS

Children are easily attracted by new things in their environment. While travelling they will find numerous 'new' objects to scrutinize and play with. Packing just one favorite toy is enough, or if there is no favorite toy leave out all of them in favor of stories or imaginary games.

## 28. CARRY KID FRIENDLY SNACKS

Create a small snack counter in your bag to store away quick bites for those sudden hunger pangs. Depending on the child's age this could include chocolates, raisins, dry fruits, granola bars or biscuits. Also keep a bottle of water handy for your little one.

>TOURIST

These things do not add much weight and can be adjusted in a handbag or knapsack.

## 29. GAMES TO CARRY

Create some travel specific, imaginary games if you have slightly grown up children, like spot the attractions. Keep a coloring book and colors handy for in-flight or hotel time. Apps on your smart phone can keep the children engaged with cartoons and story books. Older children are often entertained by games available on phones or tablets. This cuts the weight of luggage down while keeping the kids entertained.

## 30. LET THE KIDS CARRY THEIR LOAD

A good thing is to start early sharing of responsibilities. Let your child pick a bag of his or her choice and pack it themselves. Keep tabs on what they are stuffing in their bags by asking if they will be using that item on the trip. It could start out being just an entertainment bag initially but with growing years they will learn to sort the useful from the superfluous. Children as little as four can maneuver a small trolley suitcase like a pro- their experience in pull along toys credit. If you are worried that you may be pulling it for them, you may want to start with a backpack.

## 31. DECIDE ON LOCATION FOR CHILDREN TO SLEEP

While on a trip you might not always get a crib at your destination, and carrying one will make life all the more difficult. Instead call ahead to see if there are any cribs or roll out beds for children. You may even put blankets on the floor. Weave them a story about camping and they will gladly sleep without any trouble.

## 32. GET BABY PRODUCTS DELIVERED AT YOUR DESTINATION

If you are absolutely paranoid about not getting your favourite variety of diaper or brand of baby food, check out online stores like amazon.com for services in your destination city. You can buy things online ahead of your travel and get them delivered to your hotel upon arrival.

## 33. FEEDING NEEDS OF YOUR INFANTS

If you are travelling with a breastfed infant, you save the trouble of carrying bottles and bottle sanitization kits. For special food, or medications, you may need to call ahead to make sure you have a refrigerator where you are staying.

## 34. FEEDING NEEDS OF YOUR TODDLER

With the progression from infancy to toddler, their dietary requirements too evolve. You will have to pack some snacks for travelling time. Fresh fruits and vegetables can be purchased at your destination. Most of the cities you travel to in whichever part of the world, will have baby food products and formulas, available at the local drug-store or the supermarket.

## 35. PICKING CLOTHES FOR YOUR BABY

Contrary to popular belief, babies can do without many changes of clothes. At the most pack 2 outfits per day. Pack mix and match type clothes for your little one as well. Pick things which are comfortable to wear and quick to dry.

## 36. SELECTING SHOES FOR YOUR BABY

Like outfits, kids can make do with two pairs of comfortable shoes. If you can get some water resistant shoes it will be best. To expedite drying wet shoes, you can stuff newspaper in them then wrap them with newspaper and leave them to dry overnight.

## 37. KEEP ONE CHANGE OF CLOTHES HANDY

Travelling with kids can be tricky. Keep a change of clothes for the kids and mum handy in your purse or tote bag. This takes a bit of space in your hand luggage but comes extremely handy in case there are any accidents or spills.

## 38. LEAVE BEHIND BABY ACCESSORIES

Baby accessories like their bed, bath tub, car seat, crib etc. should be left at home. Many hotels provide a crib on request, while car seats can be borrowed from friends or rented. Babies can be given a bath in the hotel sink or even in the adult bath tub with a little bit of water. If you bring a few bath toys, they can be used in the bath, pool, and out of water. They can also be sanitized easily in the sink.

## 39. CARRY A SMALL LOAD OF PLASTIC BAGS

With children around there are chances of a number of soiled clothes and diapers. These plastic bags help to sort the dirt from the clean inside your big bag.

>TOURIST

These are very light weight and come in handy to other carry stuff as well at times.

# PACK WITH A PURPOSE

## 40. PACKING FOR BUSINESS TRIPS

One neutral-colored suit should suffice. It can be paired with different shirts, ties and accessories for different occasions. One pair of black suit pants could be worn with a matching jacket for the office or with a snazzy top for dinner.

## 41. PACKING FOR A CRUISE

Most cruises have formal dinners, and that formal dress usually takes up a lot of space. However you might find a tuxedo to rent. For women, a short black dress with multiple accessory options will do the trick.

## 42. PACKING FOR A LONG TRIP OVER DIFFERENT CLIMATES

The secret packing mantra for travel over multiple climates is layering. Layering traps air around your body creating insulation against the cold. The same light t-shirt that is comfortable in a warmer climate can be the innermost layer in a colder climate.

## REDUCE SOME MORE WEIGHT

## 43. LEAVE PRECIOUS THINGS AT HOME

Things that you would hate to lose or get damaged leave them at home. Precious jewelry, expensive gadgets or dresses, could be anything. You will not require these on your trip. Leave them at home and spare the load on your mind.

## 44. SEND SOUVENIRS BY MAIL

If you have spent all your money on purchasing souvenirs, carrying them back in the same bag that you brought along would be difficult. Either pack everything in another bag and check it in the airport or get everything shipped to your home. Use an international carrier for a secure transit, but this could be more expensive than the checking fees at the airport.

## 45. AVOID CARRYING BOOKS

Books equal to weight. There are many reading apps which you can download on your smart phone or tab.

> TOURIST

Plus there are gadgets like Kindle and Nook that are thinner and lighter alternatives to your regular book.

## CHECK, GET, SET, CHECK AGAIN

## 46. STRATEGIZE BEFORE PACKING

Create a travel list and prepare all that you think you need to carry along. Keep everything on your bed or floor before packing and then think through once again – do I really need that? Any item that meets this question can be avoided. Remove whatever you don't really need and pack the rest.

## 47. TEST YOUR LUGGAGE

Once you have fully packed for the trip take a test trip with your luggage. Take your bags and go to town for window shopping for an hour. If you enjoy your hour long trip it is good to go, if not, go home and reduce the load some more. Repeat this test till you hit the right weight.

## 48. ADD A ROLL OF DUCT TAPE

You might wonder why, when this book has been talking about reducing stuff, we're suddenly asking you to pack something totally unusual. This is because when you have limited supplies, duct tape is immensely helpful for small repairs – a broken bag, leaking zip-lock bag, broken sunglasses, you name it and duct tape can fix it, temporarily.

## 49. LIST OF ESSENTIAL ITEMS

Even though the emphasis is on packing light, there are things which have to be carried for any trip. Here is our list of essentials:

- Passport/Visa or any other ID

- Any other paper work that might be required on a trip like permits, hotel reservation confirmations etc.

- Medicines – all your prescription medicines and emergency kit, especially if you are travelling with children

- Medical or vaccination records

- Money in foreign currency if travelling to a different country

- Tickets- Email or Message them to your phone

>TOURIST

# 50. MAKE THE MOST OF YOUR TRIP

Wherever you are going, whatever you hope to do we encourage you to embrace it whole-heartedly. Take in the scenery, the culture and above all, enjoy your time away from home.

*On a long journey even a straw weighs heavy.*

-Spanish Proverb

>TOURIST

# PACKING AND PLANNING TIPS

## A Week before Leaving

- Arrange for someone to take care of pets and water plants.
- Stop mail and newspaper.
- Notify Credit Card companies where you are going.
- Change your thermostat settings.
- Car inspected, oil is changed, and tires have the correct pressure.
- Passports and photo identification is up to date.
- Pay bills.
- Copy important items and download travel Apps.
- Start collecting small bills for tips.

## Right Before Leaving

- Clean out refrigerator.
- Empty garbage cans.
- Lock windows.
- Make sure you have the proper identification with you.
- Bring cash for tips.
- Remember travel documents.
- Lock door behind you.
- Remember wallet.
- Unplug items in house and pack chargers.

>TOURIST

# READ OTHER GREATER THAN A TOURIST BOOKS

Greater Than a Tourist San Miguel de Allende Guanajuato Mexico: 50 Travel Tips from a Local by Tom Peterson

Greater Than a Tourist – Lake George Area New York USA: 50 Travel Tips from a Local by Janine Hirschklau

Greater Than a Tourist – Monterey California United States: 50 Travel Tips from a Local by Katie Begley

Greater Than a Tourist – Chanai Crete Greece: 50 Travel Tips from a Local by Dimitra Papagrigoraki

Greater Than a Tourist – The Garden Route Western Cape Province South Africa: 50 Travel Tips from a Local by Li-Anne McGregor van Aardt

Greater Than a Tourist – Sevilla Andalusia Spain: 50 Travel Tips from a Local by Gabi Gazon

Greater Than a Tourist – Kota Bharu Kelantan Malaysia: 50 Travel Tips from a Local by Aditi Shukla

Children's Book: Charlie the Cavalier Travels the World by Lisa Rusczyk

>TOURIST

# > TOURIST

Visit Greater Than a Tourist for Free Travel Tips
http://GreaterThanATourist.com

Sign up for the Greater Than a Tourist Newsletter for discount days, new books, and travel information:
http://eepurl.com/cxspyf

Follow us on Facebook for tips, images, and ideas:
https://www.facebook.com/GreaterThanATourist

Follow us on Pinterest for travel tips and ideas:
http://pinterest.com/GreaterThanATourist

Follow us on Instagram for beautiful travel images:
http://Instagram.com/GreaterThanATourist

>TOURIST

# > TOURIST

At Greater Than a Tourist, we love to share travel tips with you. How did we do? What guidance do you have for how we can give you better advice for your next trip? Please send your feedback to GreaterThanaTourist@gmail.com as we continue to improve the series. We appreciate your constructive feedback. Thank you.

>TOURIST

## METRIC CONVERSIONS

### TEMPERATURE

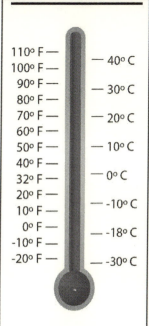

*To convert F to C:*

Subtract 32, and then multiply by 5/9 or .5555.

*To Convert C to F:*

Multiply by 1.8 and then add 32.

*32F = 0C*

### LIQUID VOLUME

| To Convert: | Multiply by |
|---|---|
| U.S. Gallons to Liters | 3.8 |
| U.S. Liters to Gallons | 26 |
| Imperial Gallons to U.S. Gallons | 1.2 |
| Imperial Gallons to Liters | 4.55 |
| Liters to Imperial Gallons | 22 |

**1 Liter = .26 U.S. Gallon**
**1 U.S. Gallon = 3.8 Liters**

### DISTANCE

| To convert | Multiply by |
|---|---|
| Inches to Centimeters | 2.54 |
| Centimeters to Inches | 39 |
| Feet to Meters | .3 |
| Meters to Feet | 3.28 |
| Yards to Meters | .91 |
| Meters to Yards | 1.09 |
| Miles to Kilometers | 1.61 |
| Kilometers to Miles | .62 |

**1 Mile = 1.6 km**
**1 km = .62 Miles**

### WEIGHT

1 Ounce = .28 Grams
1 Pound = .4555 Kilograms
1 Gram = .04 Ounce
1 Kilogram = 2.2 Pounds

\>TOURIST

# TRAVEL QUESTIONS

- Do you bring presents home to family or friends after a vacation?
- Do you get motion sick?
- Do you have a favorite billboard?
- Do you know what to do if there is a flat tire?
- Do you like a sun roof open?
- Do you like to eat in the car?
- Do you like to wear sun glasses in the car?
- Do you like toppings on your ice cream?
- Do you use public bathrooms?
- Did you bring your cell phone and does it have power?
- Do you have a form of identification with you?
- Have you ever been pulled over by a cop?
- Have you ever given money to a stranger on a road trip?
- Have you ever taken a road trip with animals?
- Have you ever went on a vacation alone?
- Have you ever run out of gas?

- If you could move to any place in the world, where would it be?
- If you could travel anywhere in the world, where would you travel?
- If you could travel in any vehicle, which one would it be?
- If you had three things to wish for from a magic genie, what would they be?
- If you have a driver's license, how many times did it take you to pass the test?
- What are you the most afraid of on vacation?
- What do you want to get away from the most when you are on vacation?
- What foods smells bad to you?
- What item do you bring on ever trip with you away from home?
- What makes you sleepy?
- What song would you love to hear on the radio when you're cruising on the highway?
- What travel job would you want the least?
- What will you miss most while you are away from home?
- What is something you always wanted to try?

>TOURIST

- What is the best road side attraction that you ever saw?
- What is the farthest distance you ever biked?
- What is the farthest distance you ever walked?
- What is the weirdest thing you needed to buy while on vacation?
- What is your favorite candy?
- What is your favorite color car?
- What is your favorite family vacation?
- What is your favorite food?
- What is your favorite gas station drink or food?
- What is your favorite license plate design?
- What is your favorite restaurant?
- What is your favorite smell?
- What is your favorite song?
- What is your favorite sound that nature makes?
- What is your favorite thing to bring home from a vacation?
- What is your favorite vacation with friends?
- What is your favorite way to relax?

- Where is the farthest place you ever traveled in a car?
- Where is the farthest place you ever went North, South, East and West?
- Where is your favorite place in the world?
- Who is your favorite singer?
- Who taught you how to drive?
- Who will you miss the most while you are away?
- Who if the first person you will contact when you get to your destination?
- Who brought you on your first vacation?
- Who likes to travel the most in your life?
- Would you rather be hot or cold?
- Would you rather drive above, below, or at the speed limited?
- Would you rather drive on a highway or a back road?
- Would you rather go on a train or a boat?
- Would you rather go to the beach or the woods?

>TOURIST

## TRAVEL BUCKET LIST

1.

2.

3.

4.

5.

6.

7.

8.

9.

10.

>TOURIST
# NOTES

Made in United States
Orlando, FL
30 January 2022